GO TURBO

KILLER PETS

TONY HYLAND

EDGE
FRANKLIN WATTS

LONDON·SYDNEY

This edition 2010

First published in 2009 by
Franklin Watts
338 Euston Road
London NW1 3BH

Franklin Watts Australia
Level 17/207 Kent Street
Sydney NSW 2000

Series editor: Adrian Cole
Art director: Jonathan Hair
Design: Blue Paw Design
Picture research: Sophie Hartley
Consultants: Fiona M. Collins and Philippa Hunt,
Roehampton University

A CIP catalogue record for this book is available from the British Library.

ISBN: 978 0 7496 8660 4

Dewey Classification: 636.088'7

Acknowledgements:
© Nature Picture Library/Alamy 33b. © Ahmad Yusni/epa/Corbis 7b & 40. © Gary Bell/zefa/Corbis 39. © Robert Pickett/Ecoscene 15. Adek Berry/AFP/Getty Images 36. Mauricio Lima/AFP/Getty Images 18. Mike Clarke/AFP/Getty Images 41b. Robert Nickelsberg/Getty Images 41t. © iStockphoto.com/John Bell Cover & 6t. © iStockphoto.com/Dusan Borstnar Endpapers. © iStockphoto.com/Sergei Chumakov 22. © iStockphoto.com/Eric Isselée 7t, 32t & 33t. © iStockphoto.com/Carri Keill 19. © iStockphoto.com/Mark Kostich 20t. © iStockphoto.com/Juan Monino 6b. © iStockphoto.com/poco_bw 21t. © iStockphoto.com/Bryan Tighe 32b. © iStockphoto.com/Zilli 8. © Natural History Museum, London 14. © Michael D. Kern/Nature Picture Library 31. photolibrary 35t. photolibrary/Ross Armstrong 13b. photolibrary/John Cancalosi 9t. photolibrary/Roger de la Harpe 16. photolibrary/Reinhard Dirscherl 30. photolibrary/Michael Fogden 3 & 21b. photolibrary/Barnaby Hall 13t. photolibrary/Index Stock Imagery 20b. photolibrary/Juniors Bildarchiv 9b. photolibrary/Darius Koehli 37t. photolibrary/John Madere 37b. photolibrary/Fabio Colombini Medeiros 17. photolibrary/Patti Murray 10. photolibrary/Nigel Pavitt 23. photolibrary/Bryan Reynolds 11. 24/7 Media/Rex Features 38. Sinopix Photo Agency Ltd/Rex Features 34. D. Roberts/Science Photo Library 12. TopFoto 35b.

Every attempt has been made to clear copyright. Should there be any inadvertent omission please apply to the publisher for rectification.

Printed in China

Franklin Watts is a division of Hachette Children's Books,
an Hachette UK company.
www.hachette.co.uk

Every effort has been made by the Publishers to ensure that the websites in this book contain no inappropriate or offensive material. However, because of the nature of the Internet, it is impossible to guarantee that the contents of these sites will not be altered. We strongly advise that Internet access is supervised by a responsible adult.

Contents

What is a killer pet?   6

Super spiders   8

Amazing inverts   12

Giant centipede   14

Stinging scorpions   16

Venom research   18

Deadly snakes   20

Tanner's Grisly Tale   24

Illegal lizards   30

Poisonous frogs   32

Captive breeding   34

Savage piranha   36

Blue-ringed octopus   38

Border patrol   40

Fast facts   42

Answers   43

More websites   44

Glossary   45

Index   46

Words that are highlighted appear in the glossary.

What is a killer pet?

Lots of people have a cute little puppy, or a fluffy kitten as a pet. This book is not about cute pets though. The pets in this book are killers.

Deadly snakes

Killer pets are only handled by skilled owners and scientists. They have years of experience and special **licences**.

Lethal lizards

Poisonous frogs

It is illegal to keep killer pets in many parts of the world because they are too dangerous. You should never pick up these animals if you find them in the wild.

Many of these pets are protected by laws. Border patrols catch people trying to **smuggle** them into countries.

Border patrol

 Look back at the contents page. Which animal do you think is the most dangerous?

Super spiders

Spiders are found all over the world. Some are large enough to kill mice and small birds. Not all spiders are good pets.

Tarantulas are the world's largest spiders. They are popular as pets. They are easy to see, because they are so big.

Red knee
Mexican tarantula

Most tarantulas are not aggressive – they are not likely to attack you. If they do bite, it will be as painful as a bee sting. If they inject **venom** you might feel sick, but you won't die!

White toe tarantula

GT Top Fact

The largest spider is the Goliath tarantula, sometimes called the bird-eating spider. It can grow over 30 centimetres (cm) wide, and weigh up to 120 grams (g).

Goliath tarantula

No one would keep a funnel-web spider as a pet, but some scientists keep them to discover more about them and to help people. Scientists have made antivenom using the venom of some creatures.

The Sydney funnel-web spider is one of 36 types of funnel-web spider in Australia. They like moist, cool places and live in silk-lined burrows and holes.

The Sydney funnel-web spider is large (the body can be up to 4.5cm), black, aggressive and has powerful fangs. The spider venom can cause a person sickness, pain and sweating. If untreated, death could occur in 2 to 3 days.

GT Top Fact

No one has died from a Sydney funnel-web spider bite since an antivenom became available in 1980.

ONLINE//:

http://video.nationalgeographic.com/video/player/animals
Search this video webpage from National Geographic (type 'spiders' into the search function) for some amazing spider action.

Amazing inverts

Minibeasts, including insects and spiders, don't have bones. Their bodies have a hard outer layer, called an exoskeleton.

This x-ray of a scorpion shows that it doesn't have any bones.

The special name for all of these creatures is invertebrates – or inverts. This means 'creatures with no back bone'.

Insects such as the praying mantis (right) have six legs. Their bodies have a head, a thorax (chest), and an abdomen. Spiders and scorpions are all part of the **arachnid** family. They have eight legs attached to their abdomen.

Stick insects aren't killers, but they are amazing inverts and many are kept as pets. They don't have weapons like the scorpion (see page 16). Instead, they rely on **disguise** to hide from enemies.

(see page 16)

ONLINE//:

http://nationalzoo.si.edu/Animals/Invertebrates
Find out more about inverts on this website, which includes a photo gallery, fact pages and information about the zoo.

Giant centipede

Giant centipedes look a bit like ordinary centipedes, but they are much bigger. All centipedes have about 40 legs. Giant centipedes can grow up to 30cm long.

Giant centipedes live in the rainforests of South America and the Caribbean, and in East Asia. They are popular as pets, but only experienced invert keepers should have them because they bite.

Centipedes are hunters. They hunt and kill insects and other small creatures. They have a set of **poisonous** pincers to kill their prey.

Poisonous pincers

Go Turbo Killer

Giant centipedes sometimes prey on bats. They hang from the roof of a bat cave, and grab a bat as it flies past.

ONLINE//:

http://videos.howstuffworks.com/animal-planet/animal-planet-videos.htm   Video clips from *Animal Planet* (search 'centipede') – one shows a centipede fighting and eating a spider!

Stinging scorpions

Scorpions mainly come out at night. Forest scorpions are dark coloured. They live in damp leaf litter. Desert scorpions are light coloured. They prefer dry sand.

Scorpions grab their prey with their giant claws and then kill it with their stinger. The most dangerous venom causes a person little pain – until later. The skin around the sting goes hard as the venom goes into the blood. If untreated, death may occur within 24 hours.

This is *Parabuthus transvaalicus* – It can shoot venom over 1 metre (m).

GT Top Fact

Top five killer scorpions:

- *Centroides suffusus* from Mexico
- *Tityus serrulatus* from Brazil (shown above)
- Yellow scorpion from the Middle East
- Common red scorpion from India
- *Parabuthus granulatus* from South Africa.

ONLINE//:

www.sandiegozoo.org/animalbytes/t-scorpion.html
Go to this link at the San Diego Zoo website for more information on scorpions, their prey and their venom.

Venom research

Australia has many of the most venomous animals in the world. They include venomous snakes, funnel-web spiders, the blue-ringed octopus, stone-fish and the tiny irukandji jellyfish.

Scientists at the Australian Venom Research Unit (AVRU) study these venomous creatures. They try to find the best way to treat anyone who has been stung or bitten.

There are many different kinds of venom. Some paralyse the victim. Others destroy nerves, or damage muscles.

Scientists take the venom from snakes to use in their research.

Go Turbo Lifesaver

How to treat a snakebite – keep very calm, and apply a wide bandage around the affected area. Get medical treatment quickly.

ONLINE//:

http://www.avru.org
Go to this site to learn more about the work of the AVRU.
There is also a fact page and a venom quiz.

Deadly snakes

Many snakes use venom to kill their prey. Their sharp hollow fangs inject venom into their prey.

Rattlesnakes (see below) are venomous North American snakes. The rattle on their tail warns **predators** to stay away.

Cobras are venomous snakes found in Asia and Africa. They rear up their heads, ready to strike.

In most countries it is illegal to keep venomous snakes, as they are too dangerous. Even the snake keepers in wildlife parks are sometimes bitten.

The Sumatran pit viper is rare, beautiful and highly dangerous.

Other snakes kill their prey by wrapping their bodies around it and crushing. These snakes are called constrictors.

The green tree python is a large constrictor. It is found in East Asia and northern Australia.

Smaller constrictors often make good pets. You can buy them from some specialist pet centres. In many countries you need a special licence to keep snakes.

Some small constrictors, such as rat snakes, king snakes and corn snakes, are popular pet snakes. These are all small constrictors, from 60cm to 100cm long.

GT Top Fact

The largest constrictors are pythons, the one below is crushing a gazelle. These grow to 2m long or more. The largest python ever measured was an Asian Reticulated Python. It was over 10m long.

ONLINE//:

http://www.snakegetters.com
Go to this site to see how snake handlers deal with venomous snakes.
There are also stories of snake rescues in the 'vet articles' section.

Tanner's Grisly Tale

Written by Leon Read   Illustrated by Kevin Hopgood

Some calls you remember more than others. The shootings, the car wrecks all blur into one – but there was this one call. I can remember it so clearly like it was yesterday.

The police radio in our patrol car crackled to life.

"Dispatch to Car 12. Proceed to 3345 Lincoln and 57th. Neighbour reports a bad smell coming from the apartment next door." I looked at my partner. He shrugged.

"Tanner here," I said. "Sure thing. We're only three blocks away."

I swung our patrol car out of the drive-thru coffee shop. We headed to the address.

So I parked up outside the apartments, in no great hurry. My partner tossed his empty coffee cup into the trash and we strolled upstairs.

"Good morning ma'am. What seems to be the problem?" I asked the neighbour.

"I'll tell you what the problem is officer. In there," she pointed next door. "Now I don't know the man, but he is cooking up something foul smelling!"

"OK ma'am. If you go back inside we'll take a look."

I knocked on the door. No answer, but I could smell something – something bad. "So what do you think?" my partner asked.

"The old lady is right. Something smells bad." I took out my baton and carefully smashed the front window. With the glass gone the smell was even stronger.

"Police officers!" I shouted into the apartment. "Hello, is anyone there?" Nothing, just silence. I unbolted the door on the inside and pushed it open. I covered my nose and walked down the short hallway.

"Jeez, what is that?" Inside the apartment was like a horror movie. Cages and boxes up against the wall. Some with live things in, others with dead things in. A huge spider's web hung across the room. I couldn't see the spider.

In the next room there were more glass tanks, and in the corner a massive snake, like a snake I'd never seen before.

I unclipped my gun.

"Don't worry," my partner said. "It's a python of some sort. A constrictor."

"Yeah, that makes me feel safer," I said, checking the ceiling for that spider.

"Looks like it's had a pretty big meal, too," he said. That's when I hurled. Spewed everywhere. But I don't tell other people that bit. There was a shoe sticking out the snake's mouth, and a man's foot in the shoe.

Turns out the dead guy was the snake's owner: an illegal pet trader. Got his punishment soon enough. The experts think he must have fallen, or knocked himself out some how. The snake just did what came naturally – swallowed him whole. The surviving creatures have been re-homed. The python has been called Hal – it's a star attraction in the reptile house at the zoo.

Like I said, some calls you remember more than others.

Illegal lizards

Many kinds of lizard are kept illegally as pets. The pet trade has brought one type of lizard close to extinction.

There are less than 200 Mexican beaded lizards (**Heloderma**) left in the wild.

Most lizards are not venomous. There are only two kinds of venomous lizards in the world. Beaded lizards are Central American lizards. Komodo dragons (above) live in Indonesia. They are the world's largest lizards.

GT Top Fact

The Mexican beaded lizard does not breed well in zoos. New projects are focusing on protecting their habitat in Mexico to keep them from extinction.

 Why do you think they are called 'beaded' lizards?

ONLINE//:

http://www.ircf.org/programs/guatemalan-beaded-lizard
Read about the work of Project Heloderma, which is trying to protect the native habitat of the beaded lizards in Mexico and Guatemala.

Poisonous frogs

Poison dart frogs are small, poisonous frogs from South America. They produce strong poisons through their skin.

Most poison dart frogs are bright and colourful. The bright colours warn other animals to leave them alone. A few animals, such as some snakes, can eat the frogs without being harmed.

The poisons in these frogs are formed from the creatures that the frogs eat, such as spiders and ants. Frogs that have been bred as pets have little or no poison, because they are not fed on poisonous creatures.

Go Turbo Killer

The golden poison frog (*Phyllobates terribilis*, below) of Colombia, is the most poisonous of all poison dart frogs. Its body contains enough poison to kill between 10 and 20 people, or two large elephants.

ONLINE//:

http://kids.nationalgeographic.com/Animals/CreatureFeature/Poison-dart-frog   This 'creature feature' is about poison dart frogs and includes a video, map, frog facts and photos.

Captive breeding

Many of the killer creatures in this book are rare or endangered. **It is not good to capture more of them from the wild.**

This scientist is checking microscope slides of animal **tissue**.

Scientists breed creatures in zoos and wildlife parks. This is called captive breeding. Sometimes they are put back into the wild.

Specialist pet owners also breed creatures such as tarantulas, snakes and poison dart frogs. These are often sold in pet shops. Some people do not agree that this should be allowed. Why do you think they feel this way?

GT Top Fact

Jersey Zoo is a famous British zoo, started by Gerald Durrell (right). It breeds many endangered animals, from howler monkeys to poison dart frogs.

ONLINE//:

http://www.durrell.org
Read about the work of the Jersey Zoo and Gerald Durrell at this site.

Savage piranha

Piranha are small fish found in many South American rivers. They are famous for their sharp teeth and their savage attack.

GT Top Fact

A school of piranha can strip all of the flesh off an animal very quickly. However, they are more likely to do this to an animal that is already dead or injured.

Piranha teeth are as sharp as razors. The top and bottom teeth also interlock. When a piranha bites it chops out a neat chunk of flesh.

Red-bellied piranha are often kept as pets. They can grow up to 30cm long. It is illegal to keep pet piranha in many parts of the world.

? Why do you think they are banned?

ONLINE//:

http://www.sheddaquarium.org/red_bellied_piranhas.html
Find out about the piranha living in one of America's largest aquariums.

Blue-ringed octopus

The blue-ringed octopus is one of the most toxic **sea creatures in the world. This small octopus is found in the Pacific Ocean, from Australia to Japan. It lives along rocky shores.**

People are sometimes stung by the blue-ringed octopus when they are looking for crabs in rockpools.

The blue-ringed octopus was once a popular pet in Thailand. But Thai officials decided that it was too dangerous, and banned people from keeping it.

The venom of the blue-ringed octopus is in its saliva (spit). It quickly paralyses the body, so that the muscles can't work. Victims cannot breathe by themselves.

ONLINE//:

http://www.aquariumofpacific.org/onlinelearningcenter/
full_description/greater_blue_ringed_octopus1
Webpage featuring facts about the blue-ringed octopus.

Border patrol

**Many animals are endangered.
People who collect wild animals
as pets cause part of the problem.**

Wildlife protection groups and governments work
together to protect endangered **species**. They have
made a large list of endangered species. No one is
allowed to buy or sell the wild creatures on this list.

Often, animal smugglers try to bring endangered species into the country, to sell as pets. Customs and border patrol officers watch out for their many tricks. If they find animals being smuggled, they can arrest the smugglers.

GT Top Fact

Smugglers try many different ways to sneak endangered animals into a country. Customs officers have found:

- spiders in plastic tubes
- lizards (right) stitched into suitcases
- pythons in garden pots
- reptile eggs hidden in clothing
- snakes coiled into stockings.

ONLINE//:

http://www.cbp.gov
Read about US Customs and Border Patrol here, plus watch videos of them at work and look at lots of action images.

Fast facts

The Brazilian wandering spider or 'banana spider' (Phoneutria nigriventeris) is the most venomous arachnid in the world.

The Goliath frog (Conraua goliath) is the world's largest frog.

Thailand is the country with the biggest number of venomous snake species: 60 of the 179 species are venomous!

The colossal squid (Mesonychoteuthis hamiltoni) is the world's largest invertebrate. The largest one brought to the surface was 10m long and weighed 494 kilograms (kg).

The most venomous land snake is the inland taipan (Parademansia microlepidotus or Oxyuranus microlepidotus) from Australia, which reaches 2m long.

A Malaysian woman holds the world record for living with scorpions. She spent 36 days in a glass cage with 6,069 scorpions and was stung 17 times.

Answers

These are suggested answers to questions in this book. You may find that you have other answers. Talk about them with your friends. They may have other answers too.

Page 7: Many of these creatures could hurt or kill you. Snakes are the ones that kill the most people every year. You are not likely to ever see most of the other creatures.

Page 21: India has the second largest population of any country. Many of the people live in the countryside. They often work with bare legs and feet, so they can be more easily bitten. There are not enough ambulances, or doctors, for the large population.

Page 31: Look at the photograph on page 31. Can you see the lizard's skin? It looks like lots of beads.

Page 35: Many people feel that these creatures should be left alone in the wild. They feel that even breeding the creatures in captivity encourages smugglers to catch more from the wild and sell them to collectors.

Page 37: People are sometimes careless with aquarium fish. When they no longer want them, they throw them out. Imagine the trouble if piranhas began to live in a river near you!

More websites

Video section of the National Geographic website, featuring reptiles, frogs, inverts and more:

http://video.nationalgeographic.com/video/player/kids/animals-pets-kids/

Home of the Royal Society for the Prevention of Cruelty to Animals, featuring information on pet care, campaigns and links to their international website:

www.rspca.org.uk

Website of Australia Zoo, featuring snakes and lizards, plus video diaries and conservation news:

http://www.australiazoo.com.au

Website of the American Museum of Natural History, featuring current exhibitions:

http://www.amnh.org

Kids pages of the Natural History Museum, which include games, videos and interviews with staff:

http://www.nhm.ac.uk/kids-only

The website of the Captive Animals' Protection Society, where you can find out more about why some people are against keeping pets and other animals:

www.captiveanimals.org

Use the search function on this webpage of howstuffworks to find videos of killer creatures, including snakes, lizards, scorpions, spiders, piranha and frogs:

http://videos.howstuffworks.com

Glossary

Antivenom – substance used to fight the effects of venom.

Arachnid – a class of animals that includes spiders, scorpions and mites. Arachnids have eight legs, but do not have wings or antennae.

Constrictors – snakes that kill their prey by squeezing and crushing.

Disguise – to hide by looking like something else.

Endangered – in danger of becoming extinct.

Exoskeleton – the hard outer shell of invertebrates such as insects and spiders.

Extinction – when a species dies out completely. Dinosaurs and many other species are already extinct.

Heloderma – the scientific name for the Beaded Lizard species. It means 'beaded skin'.

Lethal – something that is deadly. Lethal venom will kill other creatures.

Licence – special permission needed to keep some pets.

Poisonous – something that has poison in it. Some bites are poisonous.

Predators – any animals that hunt other animals to eat.

Smuggle – to hide something (often illegal) in order to move it somewhere.

Species – any group of plants or animals of the same type, e.g. the red knee Mexican is one species of tarantula.

Tissue – the substance that plants and animals are made from.

Toxic – something that is very poisonous or even lethal.

Venom – the poison made by creatures such as snakes, spiders, scorpions and bees. Most venom is injected by a sharp sting or through hollow teeth.

Index

A, B

antivenom 10, 11, 45
arachnids 13, 42, 45
Asian reticulated
   pythons 23
Australian Venom
   Research Unit 18, 19
beaded lizards 30, 31,
   45
blue-ringed octopus 18,
   38–39
border patrols 7,
   40–41
Brazilian wandering
   spiders 42

C, D

captive breeding
   34–35, 43
centipedes 14–15
cobras 21
colossal squids 42
constrictors 22–23, 28,
   45
corn snakes 23
Durrell, Gerald 35

E, F

endangered species
   34–35, 40–41, 45
exoskeleton 12, 45
extinction 30, 31, 45
fangs 11, 20
fish 18, 36–37, 43
frogs 7, 18, 32–33,
   42, 44

F (continued), G

funnel-web spiders
   10–11, 18
giant centipedes 14–15
golden poison frogs 33
Goliath frogs 42
Goliath tarantulas 9
green tree pythons 22

H, I

Heloderma 30-31, 45
inland Taipan snakes
   42
invertebrates 12–13,
   14, 42, 44, 45
irukandji jellyfish 18

J, K, L

Jersey Zoo 35
king snakes 23
Komodo dragons 30
licences 6, 22
lizards 6, 30–31, 41,
   44

M

Mexican beaded lizards
   30, 31, 45

P

piranha 36–37, 43, 44
poison dart frogs
   32–33, 35
praying mantis 13
Project Heloderma 31
pythons 22, 23, 28, 41

R, S

Rat snakes 23
rattlesnakes 20
red-bellied piranha 37
red knee Mexican
   tarantulas 8, 45
scientists 6, 10, 18–19,
   34
scorpions 12, 13,
   16–17, 42, 44, 45
smugglers 7, 41, 43
snake bites 19, 21, 43
snakes 6, 18, 19, 20–
   23, 28, 32, 35, 41,
   42, 43, 44, 45
spiders 8–11, 12, 13,
   15, 26, 28, 33, 41,
   42, 44, 45
stick insects 13
Sumatran pit vipers 21
Sydney funnel-web
   spiders 10, 11

T

Tanner's Grisly Tale
   24–29
tarantulas 8, 9, 35, 45

V, W

venom 9, 11, 16, 17,
   18–19, 20, 39, 45
white toe tarantulas 9